FLOWER POWER

Clarkson Potter / Publishers
New York

FRESH, FABULOUS ARRANGEMENTS

FLOWER POWER

REBECCA COLE

PHOTOGRAPHS BY HELEN NORMAN

To Susanne Reese, baby-sitter, friend, mother, my rock.

Published by Clarkson Potter/Publishers, New York, New York.
Member of the Crown Publishing Group, a division of Random House, Inc.
www.randomhouse.com

CLARKSON N. POTTER is a trademark and POTTER and colophon are registered trademarks of Random House, Inc.

Printed in China

Design by Jenny Brillhart

Library of Congress Cataloging-in-Publication Data
Cole, Rebecca.
    Flower power / Rebecca Cole.
        p.   cm.
    1. Flowers.   2. Flower gardening.   I. Title.
    SB404.9   .C66   2002
    635.9—dc21   2002004681

ISBN 0-609-60917-3

10   9   8   7   6   5   4   3   2   1

First Edition

ACKNOWLEDGMENTS

This book was an absolute pleasure to create. The remarkable talents of Helen Norman, Jenny Brillhart, and Annetta Hanna inspired, influenced, and elevated these pages to great heights. Helen's photography, as always, was spectacular, but it is her wit and friendship I have come to cherish most. Jenny's design brought a modern freshness to a potentially sentimental subject and her generous spirit made the work always fun. Annetta's clarity and wisdom guided this book with a keen eye and a gentle hand.

For the flowers, thanks to Dutch Flower Line and Fischer & Page for bringing such beauty and diversity from around the world to my doorstep in the wee small hours of the morning. For the million little and big things it took, thanks to Jenine Repice, Kathy Hammer, Shaqueal and Rawley Dover, Tom Richardson, Karen Partridge, and Martin Thompson of Destiny Enterprises›. To great friends who have supported and inspired me through thick and thin, thank you, Nancy Blaine, Diana Burton, Robert Verdi, Cara Palladino, Jessica Smith, Charlotte Sheedy, the Reimers, the Heneghans, and the Emericks.

I'm still salivating over Paul Begley's harvest feast, as well as the vibrant photos shot on Fuji film, the luscious prints from Print Zone, and the transparencies from Chromazone—thanks, Shazi.

To my family, which stands by me not only when all is in bloom but when things fade as well. And to Farid Boughalem, it is your passion for life, French eye, and love of all things blooming that put the power in my flower business.

CONTENTS

JUST TO INSPIRE

Nearing completion of my first batch of chocolate chip cookies, I stood tiptoe on a red vinyl and aluminum chair and asked my mom if I could throw in some apricots. Confused but supportive, she answered, "Of course." I was all of three, but the rebel within was emerging nicely. I have probably made three thousand batches of chocolate chip cookies since, but I still have no idea what the actual recipe is on the side of that yellow bag.

I know there are two kinds of people in the world: those who follow the recipe and those who toss it aside in a burst of creativity. Those of you who fit in the first group, I know you file your taxes on time, change the bedsheets on the same day every week, and are very successful. Meanwhile, those of us in the second group are still doodling on cocktail napkins in the airport bar because we missed our plane.

Regardless of your recipe-following style, if you're at all interested in creating wonderful arrangements of flowers, I hope this book will be helpful. In *Flower Power*, I have laid out step-by-step arrangement "recipes" that will allow you to follow each idea closely. But I would also encourage you to simply use these pages as a launching pad. The arrangements here are like the flowers themselves: beautiful, perishable, and fickle. They are good ideas, surely, but there are better ones around the corner. And my hope is that those better ideas will come from you.

LOCAL, FRESH, AND SIMPLE

THE SEEDS OF A LIFE WITH FLOWERS

At my grandmother's knee, I learned the rules of arranging flowers: the height of the flowers should be one and a half times the height of the vase; always use odd numbers of flowers; never mix red with pink. These rules are ingrained so deeply that even today I begin to sweat if I try to break them.

My grandfather's gardens provided us with exquisite blooms, but just as beautiful was the bounty of colorful vegetables from neighboring New Hampshire farms. The then-radical acts of adding tiny eggplants to a centerpiece and pansies to a salad made my grandmother's table the talk of town. It was, after all, a very small town. If I'd known that the seeds of my adult livelihood were being sowed at such a young age, I might have enjoyed those afternoons even more. I was too young to appreciate the rare treat of having such a vast array of nature's gems from which to create my very early floral "masterpieces."

Years later, I sat in a one-window office at the corner of Park and Eighteenth Street, in the middle of Manhattan, listening to the phone ring for the hundredth time that day. I thought of the banker who had jumped out of my window the day the stock market crashed in 1929. Every time I worked too late, the night watchman would tell me the grim story, always adding a new detail. Some nights he thought it might not have been *my* window, but the warning against being overworked and sixteen stories up was not lost on me.

That Saturday afternoon, I looked out my fateful window and felt drawn to the concrete below. I didn't want to jump, but I did want to join the throngs of New Yorkers down there who were happily browsing through the Union Square Greenmarket. They were buying fresh vegetables and flowers from the dozens of farmers who gather there to sell their harvest directly to the public. I grabbed my briefcase and rode down that elevator for the last time.

With a name like Rebecca it was not difficult to get a job with a farmer. That afternoon, I started working for John Hobarth, selling flats of annuals and cut flowers by the bucketful. The Hobarths were fourth-generation farmers from upstate New York. Theirs had been a poultry and cattle farm until mid-1980 when they began watching neighboring farms go into foreclosure on a weekly basis. The Hobarths had been selling poultry and vegetables at the Union Square Greenmarket for years, but they'd been noticing an interest-

ing trend: farmers had begun selling bouquets and flats of flowers, and were drawing big crowds. So the Hobarths converted twenty acres of pasture to cut flowers and added three greenhouses for growing annuals. Their first year in the flower business was their best in five. Three years later they dropped their cattle and chicken business altogether to concentrate exclusively on flowers, and their sales tripled. Ahh, the power of the flower.

Every Wednesday and Saturday, we—for now I was a part of the Hobarth family—sold an average of one thousand bouquets of fresh cut dahlias, daisies, anemones, sunflowers, irises, roses, snapdragons, stock, and statis at the Greenmarket. The Hobarths began work the night before, loading their trucks with buckets of flowers freshly cut from the fields and driving three hours into the heart of New York City. I met them at 5 A.M. to unload. We would sell our first hundred bouquets right off the truck to New Yorkers on their way home from nightclubs or on their way to work. I was happy with my new role as "Rebecca of Sunnybrook Farm."

The seeds of my first business were planted that summer in Union Square, and I haven't carried a briefcase since. Five years later I opened a flower and garden shop called Potted Gardens in Greenwich Village. Now, thirteen years after selling my first bunch of dahlias, I'm lucky enough to be running a floral design business I love.

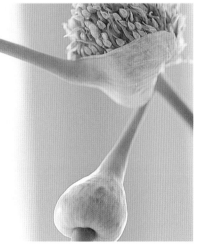

THE FARMERS' MARKET

These days, I return to the farmers' market as a consumer. I buy not only for my business but for my home as well, choosing vegetables and flowers to use in arrangements. I have found that my success at a farmers' market is in direct proportion to the size of my shopping bag and the patience and stamina of my shopping partner. For best results, go with an open mind and a cheerful companion, and remember that abundance is the key to gorgeous displays. Farmers are curious creatures, always looking for the best, most unique, or biggest variety to stand out in a crowd of common vegetables, flowers, and herbs. Look for the show-offs and search in unlikely places.

Farmers' markets and grocery stores will allow you to create arrangements that contain unique shapes and splendid colors. In other words, don't limit yourself to flower stands. In the presence of a common carrot or a humble onion, a grand idea can emerge. Whenever you're shopping for an arrangement, remember that an armful of radishes costs $5, whereas an armful of roses might cost $150. And, I would argue, radishes will add whimsy and charm to a centerpiece, whereas roses just might be too predictable.

When using vegetables in an arrangement, gently scrub them clean, leaving the outer skin intact while removing any dirty residue. Nothing will ruin an arrangement faster than the sight of muddy water or little "unknowns" floating about. For a more natural effect, try to find vegetables that still

have their leaves attached. And use lots of one vegetable, letting the plants tumble voluptuously over the edge of the container for a truly bountiful display.

Whenever farmers are involved, plan to do your shopping early in the day. Most of the farmers selling directly at greenmarkets and roadside stands have relatively small farms and plant their land carefully. Nothing can be wasted, so each week their harvests are as small as the level of risk they are willing to take in selling a perishable product. Small quantities mean that if something catches the fancy of that week's shoppers, it could be gone by 9 A.M.

By June, farm stands are full of odd, bold vegetation I can't resist. Some of the vegetables, herbs, and fruits are so spectacular they can easily stand alone as a centerpiece. Others can be mixed with the seasonal flowers that begin to bloom in abundance at this time of year. Snapdragons, sunflowers, calendula, and daisies are among the cheapest show-offs of the summer season. This is the time to take advantage of the field flowers that make perfect companions for locally grown vegetables.

And don't limit the country bounty to your table. Elegant, elongated garlic has a modern simplicity that is perfect for an office window display (left). Squiggling willy-nilly from a tall, narrow, dark-clay vase, it seems to be leaping with delight. This particular garlic will open its papery wrap to reveal feathery, flowerlike spikes after about one week in water; the display will last two more weeks if the stems get a fresh snip and the water is changed daily. Meanwhile, the long red onions match the burgundy snapdragons perfectly (above right). They'll look splendid together in a low clay vase.

Vegetables also allow you to splurge economically. Calla lilies are among the most expensive flowers available, but they might also be the most seductive. I cannot pass them by, despite their hefty price, but I've found that you don't need many to make an impact. Combining them with a vegetable allows a thrifty surprise to emerge: a vase can easily be filled in with small red onions and a few calla lilies (page 19). And even carrots can take on an almost surreal beauty when they stand at attention in a rectangular glass vase (next page).

But the most satisfying part of these spectacularly humble floral-vegetable displays is that they help to keep family farms alive. If every time we bought a carrot to eat we bought one more to display, we would be safeguarding the future of the little farm. After all, mass growers don't keep the leaves on carrots—only a farmer in love with his crop thinks to sell it whole!

BASIC CONDITIONING

If you treat flowers well, they will treat you well in return. There are very few tools and steps required to treat most flowers well. If you mishandle them, however, do not blame the poor flowers for dying too soon. Remember that they were cut from their roots in order to live in your house and make you happy. You owe them the very best short lives they can have.

Tools of the Trade

Begin any arrangement by assembling all your tools, containers, and flowers in one convenient location. Arranging flowers is much like painting. If an artist had to run to the cabinet or toolshed every time he or she needed a new paint color or brush, the work might never get done, and it would certainly not be the work of a concentrated genius.

The Essentials

Sharp penknife, clippers, or scissors
Flower freshener* or bleach
Cold water
Dishwashing soap to clean vases and tools
Plastic or nonmetal containers

A Few Extras

Rose stripper*
Hammer
18-gauge wire*
Floral tape*
Oasis*

*found in floral, craft & hardware stores

Conditioning the Flowers

All cut flowers want to be in water as soon as possible, so get home immediately. Clean your nonmetal containers thoroughly. Flowers are very susceptible to mold and will quickly decline if their container has any dirt or mold from the last flowers. Fill the container with cold water and add 1 tablespoon of flower freshener (or 1 teaspoon of bleach) for every gallon of water.

Remove all leaves on the flower stem that will fall below the water line. Also remove all leaves and petals that are dry, browning, or wilted. Remove all thorns either by picking them off one at a time with your thumb and forefinger, or with a rose stripper or penknife. Be careful not to strip too much skin off the stem while removing the thorns.

With a clean, sharp knife, clippers, or scissors, cut at least two inches off the bottom of each stem at a sharp angle. Always cut at the sharpest angle to allow maximum water absorption. Place the cut stem immediately in the prepared water. Let the flowers stand for at least one hour before making your arrangements. If possible, refrigerate the flowers at about 42 degrees until you're ready to use them. When making the arrangement, you may have to remove more leaves so that none are below the water line.

All flowers and branches with woody stems should be pounded with a hammer or sliced up from the bottom by at least one inch. This will allow the tough ends to absorb water better. Most woody stems also do better in warm water for their first hour following a fresh cut.

Specific flowers may need additional conditioning, but if you follow these basic rules you will get a good week out of nearly every cut flower, and in some case quite a bit more. And though these tasks can be time-consuming, I have never found anything more therapeutic then conditioning flowers. So have fun!

Some Simple Design Rules

Rules are meant to be broken, but my first rule in floral design is to choose a tight color palette. There are so many colors, shapes, and textures among flowers that it is important not to choose them *all* at one time. Remember to use odd numbers of flowers in your arrangements. This makes for more dynamic, less symmetrical displays. And avoid combining flowers that would not, could not, grow together in nature.

A SPECTACULAR AMATEUR DISPLAY

My grandmother was a Latin scholar who loved to teach me the roots of English words she felt were misused. In an adolescent moment I called my brother's painting "amateurish" in front of her. She bristled at the condescension in my voice and corrected me as only she could. "'Amateur,' my dear," she said, "is derived from the Latin word meaning 'one who loves.'" I quickly thought about the most common usages of the word *amateur* and realized how right she was. The Olympian spending a lifetime training for a shot at the gold, the singer rehearsing five nights a week for one local performance of *The Pirates of Penzance,* the mother baking bread for her family are all amateur practitioners of their arts. They are doing their work for the love of it.

When I first began my flower business I could only afford to hire amateur floral designers, people who had never worked with flowers professionally. All had a love of flowers, all had grown up arranging, planting, or painting flowers, but none had trained professionally. It wasn't until I hired my first professional floral designer that I learned how lucky I had been to have these amateurs to help define a unique style for my business from the beginning.

But in my second year of business I decided there were skills we were only going get from a trained floral designer. I bit the bullet and hired our first professional employee at a considerably higher salary than the amateurs were being paid. The first few weeks were grand. We learned how to wire roses into headdresses and tie bows with less ribbon. We were entertained by horror stories of bridal bouquets that were backed over by the delivery truck, and centerpieces that leaked all over two-hundred-dollars-a-yard silk damask tablecloths. We were introduced to a whole new world. All was well until my new employee began dictating which flowers went with what greens and which flowers were not acceptable in any arrangement.

At first I was so pleased with what we were learning that I didn't notice that the spontaneity was fading from our arrangements. Each one was as predictable as the last. Every flower was perfect, well conditioned, and ordinary. We had lost the humor, the quirkiness, and the charm of our early signature pieces. I tried to explain this to my colleague, but the arrangements remained the same: beautiful and predictable.

I was at loss as to how to inspire spontaneity until one day we received the wrong flowers from our wholesaler. Instead of magnificent specialty roses and exquisite anemones, two big boxes of statis and chrysanthemums arrived by mistake from the market. The delivery had been late and the market was already closed when I called to correct the mix-up. We were stuck with a huge number of two very common flowers, and two major jobs were due that afternoon. We had to come up with something spectacular. Our professional colleague was horrified that we would even consider using these "awful" flowers. Convinced that we were on an inexorable downward spiral, he walked out.

We amateurs stayed and made fabulous fun things. We came up with a dining room arrangement that was a bit of genius, using stripes of bold green chrysanthemums and purple statis to turn an abandoned fireplace into a burst of color. The added bonus is that this simple, graphic line of purple and lime green not only looks great but also will last for weeks.

STATIS AND MUM LOG

INGREDIENTS

- 2 large garden pots
- 1 long, narrow, rectangular box or file drawer
- 3–8 watertight containers to insert into the 3 containers
- Cold water
- Flower freshener or bleach
- 10 large bunches of purple statis
- 10 large bunches of lime green chrysanthemums

RECIPE

Condition the flowers (see page 34).

1. Line the garden pots and the rectangular box with watertight containers. Fill the containers with cold water and add the flower freshener.

2. Remove all leaves below three inches of the tops of the chrysanthemums. Bunch a large mass of chrysanthemums together and cut their stems so that only two inches will bob above the garden pots. Do the same with the statis.

3. Line the rectangular box with stripes of chrysanthemums and statis.

Change the water twice a week and this arrangement will last three weeks.

NOTE: The statis can be dried by bundling the stems with a rubber band and hanging them upside down out of the light. After two weeks of drying, the statis will look exactly the same, but will no longer require water.

HONORING A CHECKERED PAST

As a kid I was a doodler. I drew on my book bag, painted on my bed frame, scribbled on my friend's arm, and stenciled on my tennis shoes. No surface was safe from my Magic Markers. For one of her birthdays, I surprised my mother with a very elaborate doodle covering the floor, ceiling, and walls of our powder room. She acted pleased when she saw it—even though washable markers had not yet been invented.

The recurring theme in all my doodling was the checkerboard. I loved everything checkered and I learned at a young age that if it didn't come checkered, a little patience and a big Magic Marker could make it that way. Is it any wonder that when I saw a sectioned Coca-Cola box, I saw checkers?

Graphic arrangements work best with two bold colors for striking contrast. Here the bright celadon green of the bupleurum against the buttercup yellow of the rununculus emphasizes the graphic pattern of the checkered grid. The concept is simple: Whether you want stripes, squares, or circles, find containers that contain the pattern you want the flowers to create. If the perfect container is not watertight, like this box, simply use plastic cups to hold the flowers in water.

This kind of arrangement looks great if the pattern is clearly defined by the flowers. It's in the juxtaposition of the soft round flowers and the hard edge of the squares that this design finds its interest.

CHECKERBOARD FLOWER BOX

INGREDIENTS
- Large plastic cups, one for each section of your box
- 1 old divided box
- Cold water
- Flower freshener or bleach
- 50 rununculus, all one color
- 25 stems of bupleurum

RECIPE
Condition the flowers (see page 34).

1. Place one plastic cup in each section of the divided box. Fill the cups with cold water and add freshener.

2. Remove most leaves from the rununculus and cut low. Fill every other cup with rununculus.

3. Cut bupleurum low and fill the remaining cups.

Change the water and recut the stems every three days and this arrangement should last ten days.

A SWEET PEA REMEMBRANCE

At the sad, raucous Irish wake of my uncle Ade, there were dozens of big, gaudy, well-intentioned sympathy bouquets. He was a popular Irish doctor in an Irish town so there was quite a run on Bells of Ireland in western Massachusetts that week. But sitting just at the entrance was a tiny arrangement of all white sweet peas in a small blue teacup. It was the most beautiful bouquet I had ever seen. Exquisitely simple and powerfully sweet, it was an ironic tribute to a boisterous man. I suppose it was more a gift for my aunt Ruth Ann, since the ruffled, papery sweet pea is her favorite flower. What a memorable gesture it was.

SWEET PEA IN A GLASS

INGREDIENTS

- Paper towels
- Very sharp knife or scissors
- 35 sweet-pea stems, all one color
- 1 cocktail glass
- Cold water
- Flower freshener or bleach

RECIPE

Sweet peas traditionally grow on a vine, squiggling and turning dramatically on a thin but strong stem. In the past twenty years, however, growers have bred sweet peas that have one rather straight stem. The sweet pea is a fragile flower because it cannot retain water internally in its stem for even a short period of time; In order to transport this delicate beauty worldwide, a waterlike gelatin is placed inside a plastic bag that is wrapped tightly around the ends of the stems. This gelatin will keep the inside of the stem moist for up to four days. It should not be removed until proper conditioning of the flower can begin. When you are ready to arrange the flowers, remove the gelatin with paper towels.

1. Condition the flowers (see page 34).

2. Remove all fading or browning petals on the lower part of the vine.

3. With a very sharp, clean scissor or knife, cut each stem at an angle. Be careful not to squeeze the stem closed, choking off its ability to draw water up its open tube. If the knife or scissors are dull or sticky, the stem can close shut and the flower will not be able to drink water.

4. Fill the cocktail glass with cold water and flower freshener. Place the sweet peas in the glass, using the gentle curves of the stems to create a wide fluted shape.

With a clean cut, cold water, cool air temperatures, and the continual removal of fading lower petals, these sweet peas can last up to ten days.

ANY FLOWER, ANYTIME

THE GLOBAL FLOWER MARKET

Flowers preceded the sundial as a marker of time, a living calendar, if you will. In the northern hemisphere, if the wild anemones were in bloom, it was spring; the delphiniums signaled summer; the asters and red leaves announced fall; and the berried evergreens welcomed winter. But our ability to move goods from one town, country, or continent to another has improved so dramatically that we can barely remember what "seasonal" means anymore when it comes to flowers. Today the business of seemingly fragile, always perishable flowers is actually one of the most efficiently run in the world. A flower can be picked anywhere in the world on Tuesday morning and arrive on the other side of the globe no later than Thursday afternoon. On any given day but Sunday, the Aalsmeer Flower Auction in Holland handles 20 million flowers; 60 percent of all the flowers sold worldwide pass through its one building, which is the size of 120 soccer fields. And the United States alone spends 16 billion dollars a year on flowers, 70 percent of which are imported.

CAN IT REALLY BE SPRING?

Tulips are perhaps responsible for launching the global flower market. With its simplicity of form and intensity of color, this striking flower has engendered both passion and ruin. In the mid-seventeenth century, at the height of the Holland's Tulipmania, a single bulb was sold for the equivalent of fifteen years' wages for the average worker. By the end of that century, the Dutch economy had collapsed and by most accounts the country's obsession with tulips was to blame.

My obsession with this flower is not quite so dire, but every spring and fall my house is filled with tulips in various stages of decay. I cannot bear to throw out a single tulip before its last petal falls. In fact, my favorite stage in the flower's life is when it droops dramatically.

There are nearly as many varieties of tulips in the world as there are roses—more than two thousand

DAY ONE

DAY THREE

and counting. And now tulips are available nearly year-round. From florist shops to corner delis to the checkout lines of grocery stores, tulips can be found in abundance every spring and fall. When the northern hemisphere's growers stop cutting in early July, Australian growers are planning for a harvest of early bulbs come September. And in every part of the world, refrigeration allows tulips to be forced into bloom in summer and winter as well.

Though variety, freshness, and cost may vary from place to place, tulips are often a real bargain. When buying them for long-lasting pleasure, look for tight, closed buds. Avoid petals that are dry or translucent; this can be an indicator that the water stored in the flower is starting to drain and it may already be five or more days old. Leaves that are curling or browning at the tip are sure signs of old age. If the ends of the stems are white or shrunken, they likely have been left out of water for some time and then were not recut before they were returned to water. These flowers can be saved if the white part is removed from the stems and they are placed in fresh, cold water. Tulips with tight buds that are drooping badly will come back when treated properly; they just need a good, long drink.

DAY SEVEN

Conditioning Tulips

As soon as you get your tulips home, get a clean bucket of cold water ready to receive them. Remove most of the leaves on the stem, leaving only one or two—and only if they are in perfect condition. Make a clean, sharply angled cut at least two inches from the bottom of the stem and place the flower immediately in the cold water. Keep the flowers in a cool room and away from direct sunlight. Allow the tulips to drink for at least one hour prior to arranging them. Tulips drink a lot of water quickly and require daily refills of fresh cold water.

Straightening Bent Tulips

Sometimes too many tulips are shipped in too-small boxes. These cramped conditions can force bunches of tulips to bend. Fortunately, most will stand up straight again if their ends are freshly cut and the flowers are wrapped in wet newspaper, placed in a vase of cold water, and put in the refrigerator for a few hours. If just one tulip stem is severely bent in a group of straight ones, it is usually a sign of an air pocket trapped inside the stem. Simply prick the stem with a pin at the point of the bend, return it to cold water, and within minutes the stem should pop up.

DAY NINE

Tulips Continue to Grow

Tulips, like all bulb flowers, continue to grow even after they are cut. These Fancy Frills tulips show the life cycle of a cut tulip over the course of nine days.

A PASSION FOR ORCHIDS

As a garden designer I have always been partial to regional flowers, so when I began my floral business, I decided I'd sell only seasonal and locally grown cut flowers. By January of that first year, my naive plan had nearly buried me: there were, of course, no flowers growing in the dead of winter within a 300-mile radius of New York City! I quickly invoked my prerogative to change my mind and began buying flowers grown worldwide. That decision not only kept my floral business alive but made me a better garden designer as well. My knowledge of plant life expanded tremendously.

The only purist principle that remains in my floral designs today is that flowers that could not possibly grow together should not be arranged together. To my eye, orchids look odd with roses. Actually, orchids are so majestic, so exotic, that they look out of place with almost any other flower. They look best standing tall and standing alone. The remarkable thing about orchids is that though they look painfully fragile, they are exceptionally hardy and long lasting, both as plants and cut flowers. Because of their long stems, dramatic curves, and exquisitely shaped flowers, orchids lend themselves beautifully to simple architectural arrangements.

CYMBIDIUM IN COPPER

INGREDIENTS

- Water at room temperature
- Flower freshener or bleach
- 1 large conical vase
- Gridded flower frog
- 10 smooth black stones
- 7 monstera leaves
- 3 mini cymbidium stems (if more are desired,
  increase by twos for an odd number)

RECIPE

1. Add water and flower freshener to a large conical vase that will dramatically frame the orchids and monstera leaves.

2. Set a heavy gridded flower frog in the bottom of the vase to hold the thick stems in place.

3. Place stones over most of the frog to keep it in place once the heavy flowers are added.

4. Cut the monstera stems at a sharp angle.

5. Layer the leaves around the perimeter of the vase.

6. Cut the cymbidium stems at a sharp angle, varying the height of each by three to five inches.

7. Stick each cymbidium stem through a section of the grid of the flower frog. Arrange the stems in an uneven triangle pattern.

Change the water every two days and keep the flowers moist with a room humidifier or water mister and this arrangement will last more than two weeks.

THAT'S A HELL OF A HELLEBORE!

When I moved my business into a town house in Greenwich Village, I was faced with the challenge of a large backyard with no sun. Of course, the definition of "large" would be applicable only to New York City, while that of "no sun" is universal. Even though I had designed shade gardens for years, it wasn't until I was living with one that I realized how many plants I had been using in other people's gardens that I didn't really love. Determined to find fabulous new shade plants, I abandoned the hosta and began to court rarer species. Along the way, I began my affair with the hellebore.

The hellebore is a plant of such exquisitely subtle beauty, it hides its flower upside down in its top leaf, demanding genuflection for simple observation. My introduction to this understated gem was with the common green variety Helleborus argutifolius, with its brilliant celadon tones bringing sorely needed light to any dark garden or bouquet. But it was when I met the seductive brown hues of the Helleborus torquatus maroon variety that I truly fell in love.

Several years after the hellebore become popular with gardeners, florists discovered that its cut stems can add tremendous versatility to the most ordinary arrangements. The large, stiff, seven-pointed leaf of some varieties can effectively frame the base of a centerpiece or bouquet, and the soft open cup of its flower evokes both the buttercup and an old-fashioned rose.

A dusty rose hellebore served as the inspiration for this earth-toned bouquet. I am often drawn to brownish flowers in the market but have found that when I mix them with bold flowers of any other color, the browns become washed out. When paired with other browns, burgundies, or dusty roses, however, they are as scrumptious as mocha mousse.

With its head like an upside down tulip and its petal pattern as delicate as it is bold, the fritillaria, along with the hellebore, brings out the fickle lover in me. I claim each dazzling variety as "my all-time favorite" until its season passes and so too my affection. Then the rununculus takes my heart and all memory of the delicate, dangling painted petal is forgotten till next year!

BOX OF MOCHA MOUSSE

INGREDIENTS

- 3 aluminum loaf pans
- 1 old rectangular box
- Cold water
- Flower freshener or bleach
- Floral tape
- 20 hellebores
- 20 Sahara roses
- 10 *Iris atropurpurea*
- 7 *Rritillaria melagris* (checkerboard fritillaria)

RECIPE

Condition the flowers (see page 34).

1. Insert three aluminum loaf pans into the box to make it watertight. Fill the pans with cold water and add the flower freshener. Place floral tape across the top of the box in a grid pattern to hold the flowers in place. (I prefer using tape to hold flowers in place rather than using floral foam or Oasis, which I find gives a stiff effect.)

2. Once the tape grid is securely in place, begin building the arrangement in layers. Start with the hellebores and completely fill the surface of the piece. Capitalize on an oddly turned stem to emphasize sweeping gestures.

3. Once the hellebore is in place, add the Sahara roses in uneven but balanced groupings throughout the piece. As in a garden, roses look better in groupings than standing alone.

4. Following the roses, cut down the irises and peel back the brown papery shell underneath the blossom. This will help keep the iris from wilting before it even has a chance to open.

5. Last but not least, add the checkerboard fritillaria.

4.

5.

PEPTO-BISMOL-PINK PERFECTION

Flowers have become the universal get-well card. Many of the notes accompanying the arrangements from our floral business contain wishes for a speedy recovery. When requesting flowers for get-well bouquets, remember to ask for scentless blooms. You don't want to overwhelm the patient. Large, elaborate arrangements can also be intrusive in a hospital or sickroom. When it comes to get-well wishes, the motto should be "keep it simple."

The exquisite beauty of the scentless Pink Perfection rununculus is the ideal remedy for all aches and pains.

These magnificent little delicacies would be lost in an arrangement with other flowers, but on their own, they live up to their name. Pair these with a bottle of Pepto-Bismol, and who wouldn't get well soon?

A BEAKER OF PINK PERFECTION

INGREDIENTS

- 30 Pink Perfection rununculus
- 1 laboratory beaker
- Cold water
- Flower freshener or bleach

RECIPE

Condition the flowers (see page 34).

1. Remove all leaves and undeveloped buds from each blossoming stem. This will keep the remaining blossoms alive much longer.

2. Fill the beaker with cold water and flower freshener.

3. Arrange each rununculus separately to make the most of the tiny heads.

Change the water daily and cut the stems every 3 days and this arrangement will last for one week.

BLACK POWER FLOWERS

In painting school I discovered there was no true black. Made up of many dark pigments, it was one of the most difficult colors to mix. Achieving just the right black for an outline or a shadow was cause for celebration.

In nature, too, black is an illusion. Though "black" is used to describe a wide array of dark-colored flowers, deep, rich burgundy may be a more accurate description. And where pink and red reigned a generation ago, deep burgundy has now taken over as the symbol of true love. The Black Magic rose, black calla lily, chocolate cosmos, and black iris have become common requests for both weddings and Valentine's Day. Perhaps love has grown darker in our modern world?

The trick in using "black" flowers is to combine them with a lighter hue. I think the beauty of black flowers is most enhanced by a bright chartreuse green. Here, the startling green of the euphorbia dramatically emphasizes the richness of the black iris and the Dutch Black Parrot tulip.

It is important to place dark flowers close to a light source. I once did a wedding using all black flowers for the centerpieces. They were magnificent in my well-lit shop, but unfortunately, they were lit only by candlelight at the reception. The effect was a sea of dark blobs on white tables. I almost cried. The exquisite beauty of each flower was completely lost. What a waste.

BLACK BEAUTIES IN A DARK VASE

INGREDIENTS

- 1 small, low, square pot
- Cold water
- Flower freshener or bleach
- 8 *Euphorbia poly*
- Pot of boiling water
- 7 black *Iris atropurpurea*
- 7 Dutch Black Parrot tulips
- 15 muscari

RECIPE

Any stem that oozes a milky sap will last longer if, when cut, its tips are burned or placed immediately in a pot of boiling water. Poppies, tweedia, and euphorbia are some of my favorite cut flowers in this category. But until I learned to burn them, I rarely used poppies because they died too quickly in an arrangement. In a little flower shop in Florence, I saw a woman burning the ends of a handful of poppies. She explained in broken English that poppies absorb water through their very porous stems. If the stem is cut but not sealed off, the flower cannot absorb water and loses it through the cut end.

3

4

5

1. Fill a low vase with cold water and add the flower freshener.

2. Fill a separate pot with boiling water.

3. Cut the milky ends of the euphorbia at a sharp angle and dip the ends into your pot of boiling water for thirty seconds.

4. Fill the vase with the euphorbia stems, allowing some to flop over the edge.

5. Peel back the outer paperlike shells of the irises; the bud can rot inside the papery shell once the flower is cut.

6. Cut the irises at a sharp angle, leaving about six inches, and add them randomly to the vase.

7. Remove all leaves from the Dutch Parrot tulips. Cut the stems low and clump them together in three to five sections in the arrangement rather than dotting them evenly throughout. As in gardening, flowers look better grouped together. Sweeps of color make the most impact.

8. Finally, group the muscari together so they dance above the other flowers, adding texture and drama.

Change the water every two days and cut the tulips and muscari to keep in line with the height of the rest of the arrangement. Remove the irises when they are spent (after four or five days). In a cool spot the rest of this arrangement will last over a week.

BREAKFAST WITH MIMOSA

Gone may be the Victorian days when secret messages were sent via a code of flowers, but perhaps a more modern, ironic twist could make a comeback! When sending flowers to a particularly obnoxious politician or a pretentious actor, narcissus comes to mind. If you are just popping in for an unexpected visit, poppies seem perfect. And for a champagne brunch with loved ones, mimosa and tête-à–têtes may be just the thing.

MIMOSA AND TÊTE-À–TÊTES

INGREDIENTS

- 7 champagne flutes
- Cold water
- Flower freshener or bleach
- 15 stems of mimosa
- 50 tête-à–têtes

RECIPE

1. Fill the flutes with water and flower freshener. Remove all leaves from the tête-à–têtes and all those below the water line from the mimosa.

2. Fill the champagne glasses with the twists and bends of the mimosa. Add seven tête-à–têtes to each glass of mimosa stems.

Recut the stems and change the water daily, and these little arrangements will last one week.

1.

2.

3.

4.

FREESIA LYING LOW

There are times when the beauty of a flower is best shown simply, as in the case of this exotic crownflower with its large green sacs dangling beneath the half-open flowers. Couple it with the more common freesia of the same color, and the effect is almost as if the two flowers are one. A low glass square is the perfect vessel for this modern design.

CROWNFLOWER AND FREESIA IN GLASS

INGREDIENTS

- 1 low, square or round glass vase
- Cold water
- Flower freshener or bleach
- 1 candle
- 2 crownflowers
- 12 lavender freesia

RECIPE

Condition the freesia (see page 34). Fill the vase with cold water and add flower freshener.

1. Cut the crownflowers and singe the tips of the milky stems with a candle flame to seal off the escape of water.

2. Place the burnt stems immediately into the vase of cold water. When using a low vessel, crisscross the stems by placing one end in the water and laying the flower head over the opposite edge, careful to keep the ends in water.

3. Place the low-cut freesia in between the grid formed by the crownflowers.

4. Continue adding freesia until the vase is full.

If you change the water every other day and remove the lower petals of the freesia as they begin to fade, this arrangement will last nearly two weeks.

A DAY IN THE LIFE
OF A FLORIST

IN THE WEE SMALL HOURS
OF THE MORNING

Most major cities have a wholesale flower market, a place where flowers arrive daily from around the world and are sold to retail florists. On any given afternoon in the airports of San Francisco, New York, Chicago, New Orleans, Dallas, and Atlanta, hundreds of boxes of fresh cut flowers arrive from Holland, Ecuador, Egypt, or Colombia and are delivered to the flower market. Early in the morning in those same American cities, trucks arrive at the market full of flowers and branches from nearby farms. Most of these wholesale markets are usually closed to the general public but they can often be entered with a little tenacity and a

business card. If you love flowers and live in a large city, it would be worth your while to befriend a florist and pay a visit with him or her to your local market. Florists living in smaller cities and towns must order their flowers by phone or on the Internet; I have a great deal of admiration for these florists, who do not have the advantage of viewing their purchases in person before they buy.

Long before I opened my own flower shop I would go out of my way to pass through the Manhattan flower district on my way to work. I thought it was the most beautiful, peaceful place in the city. Little did I know that when I was passing by at 8:30 in the morning, the market's workday was nearly finished. Hundreds of thousand of dollars had been exchanged, and scores of trucks were already delivering boxes of flowers from the market's fifty wholesale flower vendors and floral suppliers to every flower shop in the tristate region. Beginning at 4 A.M. this two-block area had been packed with harried florists, cranky drivers, frenzied wholesalers, and thousands of flowers. Indeed, adjusting to the hours may be the hardest part of becoming a florist; "sleeping in" means getting started by 6 A.M., and if you begin that late, half the florists in town will already have finished their shopping.

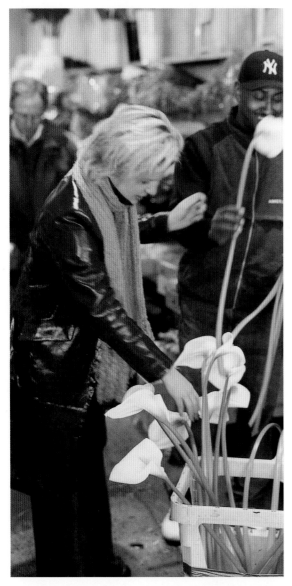

Shopping for flowers is a complex mix of economics and design. There is great variety not only in the kinds of flowers available but in the prices as well. One day a Leonitis rose could cost 65 cents, the next week it could be $1.25. When you're purchasing three hundred stems each day, that type of variation can have quite an impact on your budget. When I first began in the business I bought every beautiful flower I could afford each time I went to the market. When it came to making arrangements, however, I would have a lot of gorgeous stems but nothing that really went together. Now I shop with a list and try to keep a fairly tight color palette—and I try to remember the greens for filler. Most important, I remain open to what is fresh and well priced.

When the flowers arrive at my shop from the market we set to work conditioning and refrigerating them as soon as possible. It is important to get all the flowers into water with a fresh cut for at least one hour before they go into an arrangement. This allows them to drink up the water that will prolong their life. Refrigeration can also add as much as a week to the life of cut flowers. (See "Basic Conditioning" on page 32.)

It usually takes us about two hours to condition all the flowers. Then the fun begins. Floral arrangements for uptown homes, downtown offices, midtown lobbies, and SoHo restaurants all have to reflect the spirit of the business or the inhabitants. It's a thrilling, creative challenge every day.

WELCOMING WINDOWS

When I was a child, my parents threw some grand parties. One of my earliest memories is of looking at our house from the outside before one of these festive occasions. I stood tiptoe in the grass so my new Mary Janes would stay pristine. In the center of the picture window was a huge vase of pink roses surrounded by candles. It was magnificent! And now that I'm old enough to throw my own parties I still get a thrill when I walk outside and see a flowering display in my front window.

In the same vein, my weekly restaurant displays usually focus on the windows. They are, after all, the first impression, beckoning you inside and promising that something special will happen if you come in. When Restaurant Boughalem opened its doors directly across the street from my store, Potted Gardens, I was in heaven. A beautiful French-American bistro with all the elegance of Paris and all the charm of the West Village, it specializes in fresh, seasonal food. My charge in decorating its windows is to evoke that "just-picked" feeling.

Each Thursday morning I bring an armful of flowers and twigs and a couple of earthy containers to the restaurant. I go immediately to the walk-in refrigerator and look over the gorgeous array of fresh fruits and vegetables stored there in various states of preparation. I try to select the most common and most abundant of the day's bounty. This week I love the umber colors of the tiny potatoes and want to pair them with some budded willow in an old Chinese wooden carrier (see page 96). Inside two of the carrier's four quadrants are cylinders that hold water, flower freshener, and lots of willow branches. The two remaining quadrants contain the potatoes; they are placed on piles of crumpled newspaper so we don't waste the week's supply of tiny spuds.

One of the restaurant's windows is a bit tricky to decorate. Its ledge is narrow, only six inches wide, while the glass is five by seven feet. The piece needs to take up a lot of visual space but not much surface. Tall grasses, flowers, or branches work well.

There are two reasons to include branches in your floral repertoire: they are beautifully simple, and they make a terrific, sturdy base for large floral arrangements. Woody stems must be cut and pounded with a hammer or slit about two inches up from the bottom of the stem to allow them to drink properly. Branches do better in warm water, whereas most soft-stemmed flowers prefer cold water. When combining the two, place the branches in warm water immediately following their preparation, then wait to add the soft stems until the water cools. Branches are particularly susceptible to growing mold in water, so a bit of bleach as well as regular changing of the water will add substantial life to a branch arrangement—some can last as long as three to four weeks!

INGREDIENTS

- 1 long, tall, rectangular box
- 6 vases or other watertight vessels that fit inside the rectangular box
- Warm water
- Flower freshener or bleach
- 10 magnolia branches
- 3 feet of 12-gauge wire
- Wire cutters
- 9 bunches of Concord grapes

RECIPE

Before you make the arrangement the magnolia branches must be conditioned by cutting off all dying leaves, as well as small stems that have no leaves or blossoms.

1. Cut the cleaned stems at a sharp angle and then cut a two-inch X into the bottom of the stem. Place the stems in warm water with flower freshener. Keep them away from direct sunlight and let the branches drink for at least one hour before arranging.

2. Fill the wooden box with the vases or watertight vessels.

3. Fill each container with warm water and add the flower freshener.

4. Arrange the magnolia branches, nestling and criss-crossing one into another until the piece stays together as a whole.

5. Cut six-inch pieces of wire and wrap each around a stem of grapes. Attach the grapes to the magnolia stems just at the lip of the box. For the most voluptuous effect, use an abundance of two or three different grape varieties and let them hang low over the top of the box. Some grape clusters may have to be wired to each other.

The grapes will last five days. Once they begin falling off their stems, remove all the grapes. Remove spent magnolia blossoms daily. New buds will bloom and the branches will last for ten days.

WILLOW AND POTATOES

INGREDIENTS

- 4 vases or other watertight vessels that fit inside the rectangular box
- Warm water
- Flower freshener or bleach
- 1 grain box
- 15 willow branches
- 1 bushel of small potatoes
- Newspaper

RECIPE

1. Fill two vases with warm water and flower freshener.
2. Place the vases inside the box at two diagonal corners.
3. Cut the willow branches, then pound or slit the ends. Place inside the two vases.
4. Fill the remaining two vases three quarters full with crumpled newspaper and place in the box in the two open corners.
5. Fill with potatoes until they are almost tumbling out of the box.

The willow branches will last three to four weeks, though the potatoes will last only one week. Discard the potatoes once they get old and transfer all the willow into one larger vase. Change the water and recut the branches every week.

A FOREST LEDGE

Some places lend themselves more to "installations" than arrangements. Junno's is a restaurant in downtown New York where the food is excellent but the crowd is the main attraction. Traditional flower arrangements just won't do here. If you have a large picture window, you could use this technique at home to transform the entire window into a virtual sculpture garden.

MOSS AND MONTBRETIA ON A LEDGE

INGREDIENTS

- 20 montbretia orange
- Cold water
- Flower freshener or bleach
- Plastic wrap
- Floral putty
- Plastic inserts for terra-cotta pots, available at garden centers and floral supply stores
- 3 bricks of Oasis
- Lots of sheet moss

RECIPE

Condition the montbretia by removing most of the leaves. Cut the stems and place the flowers in cold water with flower freshener.

1. Protect your window ledge's surface with a layer of plastic wrap, held in place with floral putty.
2. Cut the plastic inserts down to one inch so they can hold water and Oasis without protruding above the moss mounds.
3. Slice the Oasis into narrow slivers and soak it in a bucket of water and flower freshener.
4. Once the water is fully absorbed, place the Oasis snugly into the insert containers.

8.

9.

10.

5. Place the containers randomly about the window ledge.

6. Drench sheet moss in a bucket of water, then wring it like a sponge till the moss is nearly dry.

7. Place the moss over the entire ledge, covering the Oasis containers and the plastic wrap.

8. Cut the crocosmia at a sharp angle.

9. Stick the crocosmia stems through the moss into the Oasis.

10. Continue to add crocosmia until the whole window ledge is full.

This installation will last two weeks if misted daily.

NOTE: Most florists can't live without Oasis. A water-absorbing Styrofoam brick, it is used to hold flowers in place while also allowing them to drink. I find Oasis both a miracle and a curse. It is ideal when using a shallow vessel for a big arrangement, but for smaller pieces it can make arrangements much too stiff. I prefer making a grid with floral tape to hold the flowers loosely in place.

THE CALLA LILIES ARE IN BLOOM

When making a showy arrangement for an entryway or a mantel, I like to use big flowers with not a lot of variety. A huge bunch of white French tulips beats a mess of twenty different flowers overstuffed in a fat vase. It was in art school that I learned the principle of clean space. A canvas full of color and line is not nearly as powerful as a canvas with a lot of clean space and a few bold gestures. Think of Van Gogh, Picasso, even Warhol. All were masters of the void, and Warhol was the master of another great design principle, the strength of repetition.

The calla lily in particular should not be mixed with other flowers. This is a flower that to me evokes a time gone by—the Roaring Twenties, when the living was grand, deco was the style, and sex and booze were the illicit pastimes. Is it any wonder that the spectacular calla lily became the unofficial flower of that decadent decade? And if there were any doubts about the overt sexuality of the calla lily, Georgia O'Keeffe took care of them: her paintings of the flower's huge snow-white head cupped sensually around the large yellow stamen made strong men blush.

When using calla lilies, the key is to keep the arrangement simple and keep it grand. The flowers are so magnificent that they are best viewed in front of a mirror so they can be appreciated a second time in reflection. The vase is crucial when working with these long, curved stems. It must be tall with a rather narrow opening at the top. This simple glass brick is perfect for the job. Its tall, long, yet narrow shape not only gives the calla lilies a chance to spread out dramatically without keeling over but allows us to appreciate the elegant curve of the stem all the way down.

WILLOW AND CALLA LILY IN GLASS

INGREDIENTS
- 1 rectangular glass vase
- Cold water
- Flower freshener or bleach
- 10 branches of curly willow
- 12 large white calla lilies

RECIPE
Condition the willow and the lilies (see page 34).

1. Fill the vase with cold water and add flower freshener.

2. Cut the curly willow branches to about one and a half times the height of the calla lilies. Pound or slit the ends.

3. Create an anchor for the top-heavy callas by criss-crossing the willow stems in the vase. When this step is completed the willow branches should look good enough to stand alone. (It is a mistake to think that this step is merely practical and need not be attractive. The willow will be fully visible and will help determine the shape of the piece as a whole. Don't

make the common mistake of thinking that a bad beginning can be adjusted later.)

4. Once the willow is in place, cut each calla stem at a
severe angle with a sharp, clean knife or clipper. This will
give the flower the best chance to absorb water and to
look neat through the vase. Begin placing the calla, working around the entire piece. As one stem is placed in the
lower left, the next might be in the upper right. The goal
is to have balance, not symmetry. Don't forget to have
some blossoms pop out in the front as well as the sides
and back.

Change the water every two days and recut the calla lilies
at the same time. They will last eight or nine days. The
willow will begin sprouting pretty little green leaves and
can last six more weeks if recut every other week. Once
the calla are removed, change the water weekly.

THE GREAT-JOB BOUQUET

Other than a raise, there is no better way to thank an employee than to send flowers. It speaks volumes not only to the recipient but to his or her colleagues as well. Keep the arrangement low and simple so it can be easily taken home. As a rule, don't give flowers on a Friday. They may be too hard to carry home and they will likely be dead by Monday.

ASTILBE AND ROSES IN A BOX

INGREDIENTS

- 1 low, square vase
- Cold water
- Flower freshener or bleach
- 7 *Pittisporum nigra*
- 11 Magic Silver rose
- 7 peach blossom astilbe
- 5 echinacea pods

RECIPE

Condition the flowers (see page 34).

1. Fill the vase with cold water and add flower freshener.
2. Begin the arrangement by intertwining low-cut pittisporum to form a sturdy grid that will hold the flowers in place.
3. Once the greens are fully in place, cut the roses low and place them unevenly around the vase.
4. When the roses are in place cut the astilbe to peek above the roses by a few inches.
5. Finish with a few echinacea pods cut low and dotted throughout.

Change the water after three days and this arrangement will last six days.

THE BRANCH OFFICE

Before spring officially arrives in the Northeast, truckloads of dogwood, forsythia, spirea, cherry, pear, and magnolia branches begin to make their way up from Georgia and the Carolinas to the flower markets. These tight buds, teasing wisps of color on winding woody stalks, are fought over by party planners and florists as if they were diamonds. There are never enough branches to soothe the chilly winter souls in the New York social scene. And just as the blossoms are in full bloom out-doors, the cut branch season begins to wind down in the flower market and its humble cousin, the curly willow, begins to shine again.

WHEN FLOWERS MAKE THE DAY

THE HEART OF THE OCCASION

There are times in life when we need to elevate and transform the everyday. We need ritual celebrations for birthdays, funerals, anniversaries, and, of course, weddings. Flowers are always central to these events. It is as if the spirit, the meaning, the heart of the occasion is captured in flowers. At these very special times flowers seem to become the expression of our soul, revealing joy, passion, and grief.

Displaying or giving flowers to mark the most important moments of the human experience is a tradition that is at once ancient and yet, because of the very nature of flowers, always fresh. Every culture has its own special flower traditions, but the universal understanding is that these passing beauties symbolize love's endurance.

A COUNTRY WEDDING
FOR A CITY CROWD

No matter how many times I do a wedding, I still get the jitters on the big day.
You'd think I was the bride, but alas, I'm
just the arbiter of her visual fantasies. It's
not the easiest assignment, but when it
works, it can be magical. I particularly
love to do outdoor weddings in the coun-
tryside. Here, simplicity is the key: not
only is it hard to beat a natural setting, it
is foolish to try.

When narrowing flower choices for
the big day, always keep in mind the
venue. A country bouquet with daisies
and mini sunflowers looks great out-of-
doors, but out of place at the Ritz. Color
is the strongest element to consider once
the style of the arrangements is chosen.
Don't be too concerned about the exact
hue of each flower. Flowers are not paint
chips or fabric swatches but living things
that contain a wondrous range of colors.

I prefer arrangements with a fairly
tight color palette and I find that bright
white flowers rarely work well with other
colors. If white must be mixed with other
colors, consider using cream and off-
white flowers instead. And as much as I
like green, I use far less of it in a bouquet
than I would in a centerpiece. Lilacs,
spirea, and hydrangeas are a great alter-
native to foliage because they provide a
background of similar textures that can
hold the piece together while still provid-
ing flowering color.

Look for interesting textures and

shapes that will set off roses or peonies. The simple addition of a few echinacea or lotus pods can turn a syrupy sweet bouquet into a modern beauty.

Keep the flowers seasonal. Remember, you may be choosing your flowers in December when that amaryllis is mesmerizing, but come June it will be just a distant memory. Flowers out of season look out of place. And though it is likely that given today's global market, you could get any flower at just about any time, you will pay an arm and a leg for it.

The Bridal Bouquet

Warning to brides: do not attempt this yourself on your wedding day. Recruit a friend or distant relative for the job.

The bouquet, if not monitored carefully, can become the object of all wedding anxieties, past, present, and future. Brides-to-be have sent me swatches of their white wedding dresses and mothers have refused to speak to their daughter-brides because they insisted on carrying red down the aisle. Remember, a bouquet is an accessory, not a member of the family. Keep it simple, match the bouquet to the dress, and don't forget it will be dead by morning.

Bridal bouquets can be as individual as the bride. The old-fashioned combination of all-white roses and lilies of the valley remains a classic but is far from the norm for today's bride. With the great diversity of style and age for modern brides and grooms, weddings have become much less formal. Bridal bouquets are no exception. The French style of loose, exposed stems cut at a severe angle has become the most requested in my business. It lends itself beautifully to any number of flower combinations and is, thankfully, rather easy to make.

The most important consideration when selecting flowers for your wedding bouquet is to

choose examples that will hold up out of water for several hours. Fortunately, that isn't as limiting as it sounds. Flowers are pretty sturdy—nature has given them the ability to retain water. Most of them, after all, traveled halfway around the world before they were even selected for the wedding.

A CREAM AND LILAC BOUQUET

INGREDIENTS

- 7 Blue Bird roses
- 3 Candy Bianca roses
- 5 Massage roses
- 3 Vendela roses
- 6 French lilacs or popcorn hydrangea
- 11 lathyeus sweet peas
- 7 rudbeckia pods
- Cold water
- Flower freshener or bleach
- Clippers
- Scissors
- Knife
- 12-gauge wire
- Rubber bands
- 3 yards ribbon
- Pearl-tipped floral pins
- Tall glass with 1 inch water

RECIPE

To provide them with the very best chance for survival, condition the flowers as soon as they arrive (see page 34).

Gather all your tools together. Once you begin making your bouquet you will have only one hand to find that rubber band you will need desperately halfway through! Have all the flowers out and ready to go as well. If you are not sure you may want a certain flower, have it ready just in case. You may want to have a friend nearby in case you need to wire a rose or cut a stem. Without a lot of practice these tasks can be difficult with only one free hand.

To begin, remove all thorns on the roses. If no leaves are desired in the final bouquet, remove all the leaves; otherwise, remove most of them. Cut all stems to about ten inches and let them sit in cold water with flower freshener or bleach in a refrigerator for at least two hours.

1. Prepare twice as many flowers as you think you will need.

2. Begin with a background flower, like a hydrangea or lilac, and loosely surround it with roses and other flowers. Repeat with another hydrangea or lilac. Continue adding flowers, with their heads facing out and their stems held in a flared circular pattern in one hand.

3. Look at the top of the bouquet to make sure it remains round throughout the process. The stems should flare out at the bottom so the flowers will at the top.

4. If there are areas in the center that need more of one type of flower, simply loosen your grip slightly, stick the flower in from the top, and pull the stem from the bottom.

5. Whenever possible, use curved stems on the perimeter so the flower head will hide the stems and the bouquet will look good from the sides. Most hybrid flowers are bred to be perfectly straight, so if there are no curvy stems, you will have to make them curvy. Do this by threading a ten-inch piece of 12-gauge wire through the top of the stem, just under the petals.

6. When the wire is pulled halfway through, begin crisscrossing the wire around the stem.

7. Continue wrapping the wire down the length of the stem.

8. Bend the stem gently to the desired curve.

9. Nestle the wired stem into the outer edge of the bouquet.

2.

3.

4.

5.

6.

7.

8.

9.

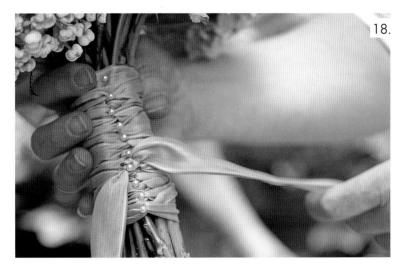

18.

19.

10. Cut the long stems once the bouquet is completed. Keep a bit of length for the final cut upon completion of the bow.

11. Secure the bouquet by wrapping a rubber band around one stem so it will remain somewhat flexible if minor adjustments need to be made as the ribbon is being tied.

12. Twist the rubber band around all the stems and complete the tie by wrapping the rubber band around a single stem.

13. Nearly three yards of ribbon will be used to tie the stems, more if a bow is desired. Always err on the side of a longer strip. You can always cut but you can't add at the end!

14. Wrapping the ribbon is a job for two people, and the one with the strong, steady arms should hold the bouquet. It takes a few minutes to make a French twist and the arms will be raised continually. Begin by finding the center of the ribbon and the back of the bouquet. Place the center of the ribbon in the back of the bouquet. Start wrapping the ribbon as high on the stems as possible.

15. In the front of the bouquet make a half twist with ribbon on each turn. Keep the twists in a straight line, close together.

16. Continue the braidlike effect for four or five inches, covering the rubber band completely.

17. Tie a double knot on the last turn in the center of the stem.

18. Pins with pearllike button heads not only will provide a pretty look but will also give a secure finish to the bouquet. Stick the pins in at a sharp angle so they will not prick the bride as she glides down the aisle. Place the first pin through the center of the knot to hold it in place. Then place one pin at the point of each twist to give the elegant effect of pearl buttons.

19. Cut off the ribbon end and the stems with a sharp angled cut. Then place the bouquet in the glass with 1 inch of water so that the liquid barely touches the stems. Refrigerate until the ceremony begins.

Modern Bouquets and Boutonnieres

Increasingly popular for weddings today are the all-one-flower bouquets. Peonies, anemones, tulips, calla lilies, scabiosa, and rununculus are a few favorites that seem to be enhanced when they are presented alone. The other trend we see is the use of non-traditional elements such as grasses, stock, or lamb's ears to update the oldest traditions.

The groom's boutonniere is one of the few occasions for a bit of self-expression on the male side of the party. The traditional one-rose pin has gone by the wayside and simpler, smaller sweet peas, lavender, and clovers are appearing on less formal lapels. The flowers used for the boutonnieres are generally plucked from the bridal bouquet, tying all the elements together nicely.

The Magic Moment

Regardless of where the ceremony is held, it should be enhanced—not cluttered—with flowers. Nowadays it is not uncommon for a bride and groom to pick a particularly beautiful church as the site for their wedding, even if it's not where they normally worship. If the church is already beautiful, don't fill it up with elaborate floral arrangements and puffy bows. Honor the style of the space with a gesture of flowers, not an explosion.

This simple Quaker hall in Vermont is beautifully accented by spirea and lilac in maple syrup buckets. Loosely hung grapevine marks the front door, announcing a special occasion, and a hint of dogwood is slid into the programs at the very last minute. The real beauty of the church is the bride, as it should be.

A Celebration to Remember

These days, brides are much more relaxed about their receptions, so the old rule of all white is no longer a requirement in flowers. I'm always happy to hear this for an outdoor reception, because white flowers can get lost under a large white tent, whereas color can really burst forth. For this spring wedding in Vermont, orange and purple were the dominant colors. Green kiwi, purple grapes, and bright orange peppers stood amid poppies and fritillaria to make the buffet table truly eye-popping and delectable.

To break up the monotony that can occur when everything matches, we designed each table arrangement with a different flower. Each of the flowers was purple in hue, so the sea of tables worked together nicely. An additional benefit—based on my unscientific research—is that a bit more mingling among guests occurs when each table has a different look.

A suitable container was chosen for each flower—sweet peas were paired with simple cream pitchers, Blue Curiosa roses and hellebores hung over a low wooden box, and lilacs with Schwartzwald calla lilies draped over a terra-cotta pot. A simple sprig of blooming dogwood was tied with raffia around each napkin and the pillar candles at the very last minute.

Tents are generally unattractive structures, but the tradition of wrapping poles and ceilings with ribbon and tulle has given way, thankfully, to more natural approaches. On this occasion, we covered the roof of the tent with loose grapevine held in place by a wire grid hung between the center poles. Votive candles placed in small jelly jars were hung in a random pattern throughout the tent. Chinese paper globe lights wrapped in grapevine added a bit more light.

The effect was one of romantic twilight. I will never forget the collective gasp as the guests entered the tent with hundreds of twinkling candles dancing above their heads. I would recommend this concept for every wedding if it weren't for the hassle of lighting the darn things twenty feet up. It's funny how weddings are planned and replanned a year in advance but often those all-important details wait until the last day. In this case, Yankee ingenuity prevailed when a contractor moonlighting as a bartender devised a long pole with a hook on the end that allowed us to light the candles and then hoist them up. The downside of this method was that it had to be done at the very last minute so the candles would stay lit throughout the entire reception. We may have waited a bit too long: the last fifty candles were lit by the two of us on the crew who were not in jeans, just as the guests were pouring in! The mother of the bride was generous enough to comment later that we added to the excitement.

I'M DREAMING OF A
WHITE CHRISTMAS

I must say I am sick of Christmas. Too much shopping, too much stress, too much *red*! I miss my mother most at Christmastime. She was a candle and fire lighter to the point of pyromania and she set one hell of a Christmas table. When she passed away over a decade ago a hitherto dormant Christmas decorating gene emerged in me. Every year my extended family comes together to share a traditional feast and my job is to make the table as Christmassy as possible. My dislike of red and green has made what should be a simple task quite difficult, but with the help of white amaryllis, French anemones, narcissus, white rununculus, silver goblets, and tall tin vases, the festivities need not suffer.

Though tall vases make a dramatic impact, they should be removed for the actual dinner to encourage conversation across the table. Frosted white pillar candles illuminate the little snow-white centerpieces. Each individual flower can be appreciated more when displayed separately and cut low so just its head is viewed.

A SILVER WHITE TABLE

The concept for this table display is one type of flower per vase. Not only is this a simple solution to decorating the room but it also allows each flower to be appreciated without the distraction of another beauty too close by. Vases of similar materials and flowers of all one color create a dramatic table with all the warmth of a traditional Christmas centerpiece.

INGREDIENTS

- Cold water
- Flower freshener or bleach
- Water pitcher with a narrow spout
- 12 small silver vases in a variety of shapes
- 30 white French anemones
- 50 white narcissus
- 25 white rununculus
- 12 white amaryllis
- 7 tall tin vases

RECIPE

Condition the flowers (see page 34).

1. Fill each vase with cold water and flower freshener.

2. Cut the anemones, narcissus, and rununculus low so their heads just peek out over the various vases.

3. Leave the amaryllis stems long because they will provide the height and drama needed for a grand dinner.

4. Amaryllis drink by absorbing water from the inside of their long stems. Turn them upside down and, using a pitcher with a narrow spout, pour water directly into the stem. This will make the flower last days longer.

5. Hold your thumb over the cut end so the water in the stem won't drain out before it hits the water in the tall tin vase.

Change the water daily in small cups and every two days in large ones. All these flowers will last at least one week if kept out of direct sunlight.

THE ST. VALENTINE'S DAY "MASSACRE"

A couple of years ago I stupidly changed flower vendors the week before
Valentine's Day. My new vendor promised me a great deal on red roses if I
bought several thousand and ordered early. Still new to the business, I
agreed. On February 13, late in the afternoon, my roses arrived. Their tiny,
pointy, dried-up, brown heads looked as if they hadn't had a drink in weeks.
Two thousand stems not fit for the Addams Family. I cried and screamed
and considered murder, then suicide, then tulips. Who said roses were the
only romantic flower? Who ever promised me a rose garden, anyway? Why
not spice things up a bit with a nontraditional bouquet? So we did and it
worked. We ended up with more business that year than any year prior.
Most wooers said they were tired of giving roses and liked the idea of being
a bit more original.

Years later we are still offering two dozen tulips on Valentine's Day for the "original" romantic. After all, when flowers are more unique, or sweet, or spectacular than most, recipients will attribute more love, more spontaneity, more creativity to the gesture. If not tulips, why not rununculus or calla lilies or something else out of the ordinary?

And if you are a traditional lover and must send roses, send them with a twist. How about wrapping them in the *New York Times* wedding announcements? This is, after all, the day to take a risk, not the day to be practical.

CELERY AND ROSES FOR DINNER

With our fast-paced lives, long commutes, and heavy workloads, the formal dinner party has nearly become a thing of the past. I have fond childhood memories of setting out the "good" china and the "real" silverware for my parents' dinner parties. My mother would spend two days preparing the canapés, the roast, the casseroles, the pies, and the decor. It is a wonder we refer to those days as simpler times: entertaining was far from simple.

Nowadays dinner parties are more likely to occur when business associates or friends stay late enough that stomachs begin to grumble and take-out menus spontaneously appear. Just because the formal dinner party has fallen by the wayside, our dining rituals need not feel deprived of festivity. When the bag of boxed food arrives, flowers on the table can still elevate the mood. And if you're not cooking, why not use food in the centerpiece to give the meal that straight-from-the-kitchen feel? With ingredients as simple as celery and roses, you can whip up something quite last-minute and very special.

A BOWL OF CELERY AND ROSES

INGREDIENTS

- Cold water
- Flower freshener or bleach
- 1 large salad bowl
- 2 bunches (20 stalks) of celery
- 20 Toscana roses

RECIPE

Condition the flowers (see page 34).

1. Pour cold water and flower freshener into a large salad bowl.

2. Separate and clean the celery stalks.

3. Cut off the short, leafy celery stalks and save them.

4. Place long stems of celery in a crisscross grid in the bowl, keeping holes open in the celery grid.

6.

5.

7.

5. Place the leafy celery tips throughout the center of the bowl in between the larger stalks.

6. Continue to add celery until the bowl is full of green celery tips.

7. Cut the roses short.

8. Gently force the petals to open.

9. Position the roses securely between celery leaves and stems. Order Chinese take-out and invite your friends to stay.

Change the water by taking the bowl to the sink and filling until it over-flows. This arrangement will last for one week.

TEA WITH NO SYMPATHY

If my brother Jeff hadn't married a Southern girl I might never have learned the high art of the afternoon tea. My first exposure to a high tea was in the form of the grand Southern tradition of the "Trousseau Tea." It is traditionally held five days before the wedding, and women only are invited to the mother of the bride's home at 4 P.M. The original purpose for such an event was to view the gifts, the wedding dress, the travel clothes, and the nuptial lingerie. At my sister-in-law's tea, the one hundred women seemed more interested in socializing than anything else. It was a fabulous combination of high tradition and down-home Southern hospitality. I leaned toward the latter but admired the flower arrangements made in silver bowls that matched the tea service!

1.

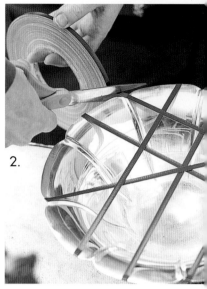

2.

3.

4.

5.

6.

TEA ROSES IN A SILVER BOWL

INGREDIENTS

- Cold water
- Flower freshener or bleach
- Silver bowl
- Floral tape
- 20 spray roses
- 30 muscari

RECIPE

Condition the flowers (see page 34).

1. When the mouth of a container is too large to hold flowers in place, Oasis, frogs, and floral tape are good options; my favorite is tape. Dry the outer edge of the bowl or vase thoroughly so the tape will adhere well. Place the tape in a grid pattern evenly across the opening.

2. End the tape a half inch below the surface of the bowl. Too much tape will be visible down the sides, but too little won't hold.

3. Once the tape is securely in place fill the vase with cold water and add flower freshener. Cut the spray roses low and fill the vase, making sure a nice amount falls over the edge.

4. Remove leaves from the muscari and cut low.

5. Add the muscari in uneven clumps throughout the roses.

6. Save the leaves of the muscari to create a simple accent arrangement.

Change the water by holding the bowl under the sink and filling it until old water is completely replaced. This arrangement will last one week.

153

PICK YOUR OWN

SPECTACULARLY SIMPLE

I can still taste the breakfast I was served twenty years ago when visiting a friend on her farm. Summoned early, I arrived at the table at 6 A.M., groggy and a bit put out to see nothing more than a pot of boiling water on the stove. My friend asked me to follow her out the kitchen door to the chicken coop, where we collected a half dozen still-warm eggs. We returned by way of the vegetable patch, where we stopped to pick some ears of corn and a head of lettuce. Just in front of the kitchen door I snipped a dozen snapdragons and made a centerpiece while my friend shucked the corn. Five minutes later we were eating the best breakfast I've ever had, at the prettiest table I've ever seen.

That breakfast is the standard by which I now measure all breakfasts. And surprisingly, in the heart of New York City, I can come close to re-creating that feeling by walking out my apartment door to gather fresh produce and flowers.

MILK, EGGS, AND FLOWERS

When I first opened my flower and garden shop my biggest competition was the beautiful, well-priced, and well-stocked Korean delis that stand on just about every corner of New York City. There, every flower and fruit imaginable is available any time of day or night. Certainly most business-school graduates would discourage anyone from opening a flower shop with that type of competition. And they may be right. In my first year in business I tried to match them by selling common flowers at low prices. That approach definitely didn't work. The Korean grocers had been doing this a lot longer; they were a lot smarter and a lot cheaper. They have been observing New Yorkers' shopping patterns for a half century and have adapted to each shift. Their small selection of flowers in the 1980s gave way to a large, sophisticated array of unique and inexpensive petals and greens in the 1990s.

When I found myself tempted to buy flowers at these shops, even as the owner of a flower shop, I knew I had a problem on my hands! I decided to concentrate my business on the *arranging* of flowers and on special events, weddings, and restaurant and corporate accounts. It was a good shift, for I was no longer dependent on day-to-day flower sales.

Midway through the nineties, suburban grocers caught on to the American consumer's growing appetite for flowers. Major grocery-store chains began making cut flowers available year-round, and if you could stay away from the prearranged bouquets, the selection was not bad. It was as if we were becoming French. Along with our weekly rations of bread, milk, and eggs, we now needed flowers to sustain us.

Today just about anyone in America can buy inexpensive cut flowers. The key to arranging them is to edit well. Abundant amounts of just a few varieties can be most successful. When shopping at a deli or grocery store, look for the least expensive, strongest flower and buy an armload. I would skip the roses at these venues, since they are generally of a lower grade and may not open. Stick with sunflowers, irises, daffodils, snapdragons, and dahlias. They can be as good as those in any expensive floral shop.

Whether shopping for flowers in a grocery store or a flower shop, look for signs of age. Crumpled wrapping, rotted leaves, and the fact that there is only one bunch left could all be signs that the shipment arrived a week ago. No matter how cheap they are, don't buy old flowers. As bad as they look now, they will look ten times worse after spending time in a hot car inside a plastic bag and out of water.

A PITCHER OF SUNFLOWERS

The beauty of a simple arrangement begins with the selection of an appropriate vase. The color and shape of the vase is as important as the choice of flowers. Common sunflowers can be breathtaking in a golden yellow oversized water pitcher from Provence.

INGREDIENTS

- Cold water
- Flower freshener or bleach
- 1 pitcher
- 15 sunflowers
- 12 solidaster

RECIPE

Condition the flowers (see page 34).

1. Fill the vase with cold water and add flower freshener.
2. Remove all the leaves from the flowers.
3. When working with thick, heavy flowers such as sunflowers, begin the arrangement by cutting the stems down so their heads rest on and droop over the edge of the vase. Closely pack the flowers for a sumptuous display and add the thinner stems of the solidaster last.

Change the water and cut the stems a full inch every three days and this arrangement will last ten days.

TRIBUTE TO VAN GOGH

Van Gogh elevated the iris to almost mythical proportions. Fortunately, this bulb is so easy to grow and multiplies so quickly that even with its masterpiece status, it remains an affordable flower. The only difficulty in working with irises is that they can open too quickly and have a rather stiff stem. Always buy irises completely closed, since they will open the minute they hit the water. Combine them with a curvy, floppy green like *Viburnum opullus* to give the illusion that the iris is bending.

IRISES IN A BLUE JUG

INGREDIENTS

- Pottery vase or jug
- One-gallon plastic soda bottle
- Box cutter
- Cold water
- Flower freshener or bleach
- 7 *Syringha vulgaris* lilac
- Hammer
- 12 *Viburnum opullus*
- 20 Blue Magic irises
- 10 poppy pods

RECIPE

Condition the flowers (see page 34).

1. Most old pottery jugs are too porous to hold water, so a one-gallon plastic soda bottle makes an ideal watertight insert. Cut off the upper section with a box cutter and place it inside the jug. Fill the plastic bottle with cold water and flower freshener.

2. Remove all the leaves from the lilac branches and cut the stems so that only the petals will show above the rim of the vase. Pound the bottom of the lilac stems with a hammer. Do the same with the viburnum and add to the arrangement. Cut irises on a sharp angle and place in arrangement.

3. Complete the arrangement with the poppy pods.

Change the water every three days and remove spent flowers daily. This arrangement will last one week.

A FEAST TO BEHOLD

Since history was first recorded, and no doubt before that, every culture has celebrated the fall harvest. For some, it is the most sacred of occasions. Every year on a farm forty miles outside of Baltimore where my photographer, Helen Norman, lives with her family, the harvest is celebrated in the middle of the field with hearty food and good friends. At the end of a long, hot summer we did our part to honor this tradition as we welcomed in the broccoli and Brussels sprouts with fine wine, lots of laughs, and a golden sunset.

When nature is the backdrop, simplicity should rule. With hay bales for seating and flowers that matched the harvest colors, the mood was set. Old friends and family gathered in the barn for iced tea and cocktails. As the sunlight streamed through the slats in the barn, friends we hadn't seen all summer shared stories of their adventures and vacations. Before the sun went down, three pickup trucks carried food, flowers, wine, and a harvest table to the broccoli fields below.

It is always my job to bring the flowers for Helen's harvest party, and my number one objective when I go to the market in New York is *simplicity*. I don't want to arrive with buckets of flowers after my four-hour drive south and have to prepare complicated arrangements before the sun goes down. Once I have selected the flowers, I pass by my home and pick up various vessels and vases. Each type of flower or green should have its own simple country pitcher, bucket, or box. In the groupings of these single-flower arrangements, a truly spectacular display emerges.

MATCHING ONE FLOWER TO ONE JUG

INGREDIENTS

- 6 various country containers such as pitchers and buckets
- 20 *Alchemella mollis* (lady's mantle)
- 24 Leonitis or Cleopatra roses
- 20 sprigs dill
- 10 *Asclepia pysocarpa*
- 20 mini gerbera daisies
- 10 montbretia pods

RECIPE

Condition the flowers as described on page 34.

1. Match each type of flower to a pitcher or bucket of the appropriate size and shape.

2. Fill each container with cold water and flower freshener. Fill each with just one type of flower, except for the gerbera daisies, which won't stand up without some help.

3. Make a structural base for the daisies with the montbretia pods.

4. Make arrangements by grouping pitchers and buckets together, emphasizing the various heights, shapes, and colors.

Change the water every other day and most flowers will last one week.

168

AN ORANGE DAISY PITCHER

Gerbera daisies seem common enough flowers. But their brilliant colors combined with their perfect dark centers make them extraordinary. I love to use gerbera daisies with other bold flowers such as calla lilies, chrysanthemums, or carnations. They don't work as well with romantic flowers in subtle tones such as roses, peonies, or rununculus. The absolute best way to show off gerbera daisies is to let them stand alone. Choose a vase that complements the color of the flower and keep the stems longs: the vivid, mod head will seem to dance at the tip of its curvy long stem.

GERBERA DAISIES IN AN ENAMEL PITCHER

INGREDIENTS

- 1 enamel water pitcher
- Cold water
- Flower freshener or bleach
- 10 montbretia pods
- 20 gerbera daisies

RECIPE

Condition the flowers (see page 34).

1. Fill the pitcher with cold water and flower freshener.

2. Cut the montbretia stems so that the curved tops with the pods will hold the gerbera daisies up high above the ledge of the pitcher. Leave the stems of the gerbera daisies as long as possible and let their heads rest on the montbretia stems.

ARRANGING TERRA-COTTA

I remember quite distinctly the first time I saw the Leonitis rose. It was back in the days when I had an office job and a pregnant colleague received an arrangement from her husband every week. Every Monday afternoon, a fish-bowl of pink or red roses was delivered to the reception desk. The first few weeks we oohed and ahed over the very sweet gesture. But as the months went on we barely noticed—until the day the most exquisite terra-cotta-colored roses came. All that week, the burnt orange petals created a rusty sunset on my friend's desk. None of us had ever seen anything like them before. We called the florist and asked her for the name of the rose. She told us it was Leonitis.

Now there is no rose I use more frequently. Over the years I have probably arranged 50,000 Leonitis roses into every conceivable bouquet. I'm a big fan of texture in arrangements, particularly when using roses. Next to the near black of the center of a sunflower, these roses take on an almost surreal look.

When working with a flower as spectacular as the Leonitis rose, keep the palette warm and close to the burnt orange of the outer petals. This bouquet contains the almost iridescent orange of the echinacea seedpod, the coral of the hyperacid, the orange-tipped seedpods of the montbretia, the mossy green of the broccoli leaves, and the deep, saturated browns of the center of the sunflower. The yellow sunflower petals were too bright, too competitive with the subtle hues of the Leonitis, so I removed each petal, leaving only the dark centers.

One of my favorite inexpensive and versatile vases is a low terra-cotta pot. Of course, it is porous and usually comes with a hole in the bottom, so it won't hold water. To make it watertight, another container needs to be placed inside it.

For a fall harvest party, huge, deep green broccoli leaves picked fresh from the field serve as the perfect complement to both the pot and the flowers. But don't let the massive size of the broccoli leaves fool you; they are very fragile. They will tear and wilt easily, so place the entire stock in cold water minutes after you pick it.

LEONITIS IN A
TERRA-COTTA POT

INGREDIENTS

- 1 galvanized pail to hold water
- 1 terra-cotta pot
- Cold water
- Flower freshener or bleach
- 11 Leonitis roses
- 5 Sensual roses
- 8 sunflowers
- 9 echinacea seedpods
- 10 Pinky Flair hypericum
- 11 montbretia stems
- 4 broccoli leaves

RECIPE

Condition the flowers as described on page 34.

1. Place the pail in the terra-cotta pot and fill it with cold water and flower freshener.

2. Begin the arrangement by filling the pot with Leonitis and Sensual roses cut short enough that no stem will show over the edge of the pot.

3. Arrange all the roses before moving on to the next flower.

4. Remove all the leaves and petals of the sunflower.

5. Cut the stems low.

6. Place the head of the sunflowers randomly throughout the arrangement, allowing some to droop over the edges of the pot.

7. Add the echinacea pods and hypericum berries. Cut evenly with the roses and sunflowers.

8. Cut the montpretia pods so that they will dance above the heads of the roses.

Change the water every two days and this arrangement will last one week.

CONTAINING A BOUNTIFUL HARVEST

INGREDIENTS

- 4 watertight inserts
- 1 divided grain box
- Cold water
- Flower freshener or bleach
- 3 artichokes with stems
- 25 Orange Princess tulips
- 12 *Alchemella mollis*
- 25 tulips of all one color

RECIPE

Condition the flowers (see page 34).

1. Tuck a watertight container into each quadrant of an old divided box.

2. Add cold water and flower freshener.

3. Place one color of tulips in one container, letting them hang over the edge.

4. Cut the artichoke stems low and place them in another container.

5. Do the same in the remaining containers with the alchemella and the second bunch of tulips.

Change the water in each container every two days and cut the tulips one inch at the same time. This arrangement will last one week.

INDEX

Page numbers in *italics* refer to photographs.

IN HONOR OF ...

It is a lucky thing I get to work with flowers every day. Strong and fragile, they hold the mystery and beauty of life. All of us were reminded of the strength of the human spirit and the fragility of life on September 11, 2001. In the weeks following, I would pass by the firehouse at the end of my block and pause before the dozens of fresh flowers left each day by strangers to honor the eleven men who had died to save people they did not know. Amazingly, there never seemed to be a wilted or dead flower among the bouquets. It was a constant reminder of the power of love.